AF584958

# UP!

Charles Hope

First published in 2021 by

Abbotsford Convent
1 St Heliers Street
Abbotsford, Vic 3067
Australia
wdog.com.au



Printed and bound in China by Everbest Ltd.

ISBN: 9781742035918

Wild Dog would like to thank Alex Catto-Smith for his careful fact checking, and Neil Conning for his thorough proofreading.

10 9 8 7 6 5 4 3 2 1    21 22 23 24 25

A catalogue record for this book is available from the National Library of Australia

FSC® is a non-profit international organisation established to promote the responsible management of the world's forests.

PHOTO CREDITS:
Front cover Vaclav Volrab; p 1 Sergey Nivens; p 2 petovarga; pp 4-5 intararit; p 6 (turbine) Suwin; p 6 (generator) ProstoSvet; p 6 (refinery) Red ivory; p 7 (gas) yuratosno3; p 7 (wood) k_samurkas; p 7 (fire) Solodov Aleksei; p 7 (wind turbines) biletskiyevgeniy.com; p 8 alexandre zveiger; p 9 (offices) Creative Lab; p 9 (containers) Travel mania; p 9 (car) Jenson; p 10 mimagephotography; p 11 Romariolen; pp 12-13 (timeline) Aleksandr Bryliaev; p 12 (fire) Victor Z; p 12 (sun) Hikiray; p 12 (oil) nendra wahyu kuncoro; p 12 (boat) Creative icon styles; p 12 (coal) Kilroy79; p 13 (magnifying glass) panda_o; p 13 (windmill) Leo Kavalli; p 13 (cow) studio haseba; p 13 (torch) natrot; p 14 Everett Collection; p 16 (HAWT) imagevixen; p 16 (VAWT) Joseph Sohm; p 17 Coral Brunner; p 18 Anna Vaczi; p 19 Dmitry Pichugin; pp 20-21 (arrow line) Dee Angelo; p 20 (01) Parilov; p 20 (02) Brad Sauter; p 20 (03) James Marvin Phelps; p 20 (04) Kodda; p 20 (05) asharkyu; p 20 (06) SmartS; p 21 (07) hramovnick; p 21 (08) only_kim; p 21 (09) Pand P Studio; p 21 (10) Geza Farkas; p 21 (11) ChrisVanLennepPhoto; p 21 (12) Rhonda Roth; p 21 (13) Ben Jeayes; p 23 crbellette; p 24 Visions-AD; p 25 Johann Ragnarsson; p 26 Doug McLean; p 27 Joel Everard; pp 28-29 VectorMine; p 29 (various) Cube29; pp 30-31 kirillov alexey; Back cover huyangshu; p 15 "Public health: industrial workplace", CC BY 4.0, Public Domain (source unknown); p 22 Public Domain / NASA.

# CONTENTS


Introduction 4-5
Primary & secondary 6
Renewable & non-renewable 7
How is energy used? 8-9
Energy and power 10-11
Energy over time 12-13
The Industrial Revolution 14-15
Wind 16
Solar 17
Nuclear 18
Fossil fuels 19
From source to you 20-21
Hydrogen 22
Hydroelectricity 23
Biomass 24
Geothermal 25
Tidal 26
Wave 27
Climate change 28-29
The future of power 30-31
Glossary 32
Index 32

# INTRODUCTION

Humans need energy to move. This energy comes from the food we eat. Machines and appliances also need energy to move. This comes from a range of energy sources.

Not all energy sources are equal. Some energy sources are plentiful, reliable and inexpensive to use, though they may be damaging to human and environmental health. Others can be unreliable, difficult to access and costly to convert into useable energy, but these sources may contribute much less pollution to the atmosphere.

As humans leave an increasingly heavier footprint on the Earth, our relationship with energy needs to be carefully considered. Which energy sources will run out and when? Which will be available for years to come? Which are the most harmful to the environment and which will not contribute to climate change? Which existing sources have yet to reach their potential, and are there new sources waiting to be discovered?

One thing is for sure: energy is fundamental to modern life. Without it, there would be no air conditioning, no internet, no phones, no cars and no television. Much of our food and drink would no longer exist. Our lives would be completely different.

# PRIMARY & SECONDARY

Energy can come from a primary or a secondary source.

Primary sources, such as fossil fuels (oil, coal and natural gas), nuclear fuels, solar, wind, water, biomass and geothermal energy, can be used in their original state. They do not need to be transformed before their power can be used.

A secondary energy source is produced when primary sources undergo transformation.

*Turbine*

Electricity can be made from most primary sources, but first it needs to be generated. This is usually done using turbines. Turbines are a type of engine that turn fluid movement into energy. They have a rotor with blades attached, and when fast-moving fluids such as air, steam or water from primary energy sources push on the blades, the blades rotate and turn the rotor. The rotor is connected to a generator, which converts the movement of the rotor into electricity. This electricity is then ready to be used in homes and other buildings.

*Fuel-powered generator*

Generators come in different sizes. If there is no reliable power source, such as in a remote area or for a mobile home, you might have your own small generator. Or they can be huge and used to generate power on a massive scale, which is then stored and delivered to towns or cities or large-scale factories.

*Oil refinery*

When crude oil is extracted it has impurities. Before oil can be turned into petrol and other products, these impurities must be removed. This is done by heating the oil and separating the bits that aren't wanted. This process is known as ***refining***.

# RENEWABLE & NON-RENEWABLE

Energy sources can be non-renewable or renewable.

Non-renewable energy sources are finite. Examples include coal, natural gas, oil and nuclear fuels, which take millions of years to replace themselves.

*Natural gas flame*

Renewable energy sources constantly replace themselves. Examples include solar, water, wind, biomass and geothermal.

Energy from the sun, wind, water and geothermal energy are inexhaustible. Biomass takes time to grow but can be replaced within a human lifetime.

*Wood is an example of biomass*

Non-renewable energy sources are cheap, plentiful and easy to convert to energy, though one day they will run out. Fossil fuels are made primarily of carbon, and burning them releases huge amounts of carbon dioxide into the atmosphere. Mining for them also damages the environment.

Renewable energy sources are often referred to as ***clean energy***, as they don't produce carbon dioxide. Less pollution is better for human health and the environment. Arguments against renewables are the high cost of infrastructure and that sources such as wind and solar are 'unreliable'.

*Burning fossil fuels is harmful to the environment*

*Wind power is an example of clean energy*

# HOW IS ENERGY USED?

We consume energy daily. The clothes we wear, the devices we use and the food we eat all require energy in their manufacturing process.

Right now, as you are reading this book, are there lights on? Can you see any televisions, computers or interactive whiteboards? Is there heating or air conditioning controlling the temperature?

Energy consumption is not limited to your school. The four needs for energy are residential, commercial, transport and industry.

***RESIDENTIAL***
In our homes, energy is used for lighting, temperature control, hot water, cooking, televisions and computers.

*COMMERCIAL*
These are retail and service buildings, such as schools, shops, offices, hospitals, shopping centres and sports stadiums.

Commercial buildings use energy in similar ways to residential.

*TRANSPORT*
Transport is dependent on energy consumption. This includes personal vehicles, public transport, freight and delivery vehicles, tourism and pipelines. Nearly everything we use on a daily basis requires transport to get to us.

*INDUSTRY*
This sector is responsible for making essential products we use every day. Industrial processes use large amounts of energy.

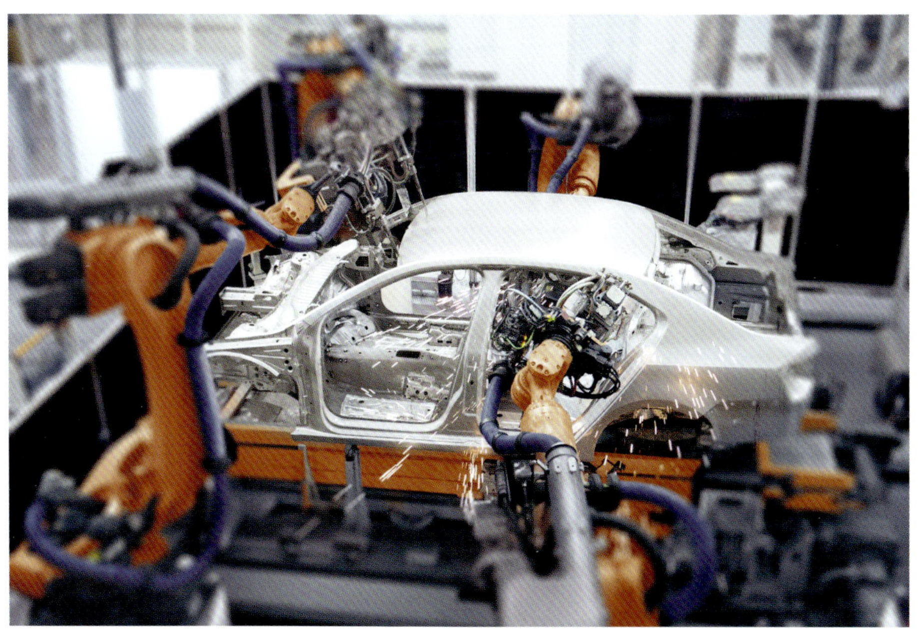

# ENERGY AND POWER

The words 'energy' and 'power' are often used to refer to the same thing.

Energy is the ability to do work. In physics, work is defined as the exertion of force and the movement it causes. This can be expressed as Work = Force × Distance.

Let's say it normally takes you 10 minutes to walk 1 kilometre. An amount of energy is used to move your legs and the resulting force moves your body.

The standard unit of human energy is the joule (J). In electricity production, joules are measured in kilowatt-hours (kWh). One kWh is equal to 3.6 megajoules, or 3.6 million joules.

Power is the rate at which work is done. Another way of saying this is power is the rate at which energy flows. This can be understood as Power = Work ÷ Time.

Let's say you travel twice as fast when running i.e. it took 5 minutes to run one kilometre instead of 10 when walking. Assuming no other losses, the same amount of energy would be used but with twice the amount of power.

The standard unit of power is the watt (W). One watt is equal to one joule per second. The amount of energy a country consumes is often measured in gigawatts (GW). One GW is equal to 1 billion watts.

# ENERGY OVER TIME

In the past, humans had fewer energy options. They ate food so they could work and survive. They obtained thermal energy from the sun and from fire. Controlled fire led to cooking, which meant more energy could be extracted from food.

In the last five to six thousand years, people have learned to harness the energy from more sources.

**5TH CENTURY BCE**

The Athenian playwright Aristophanes mentions a "magnifying device" that is used to make fire in his comedy *The Clouds*.

**5TH–9TH CENTURIES CE**

Waterwheels and windmills began to be used in Iraq, Iran, Egypt and China.

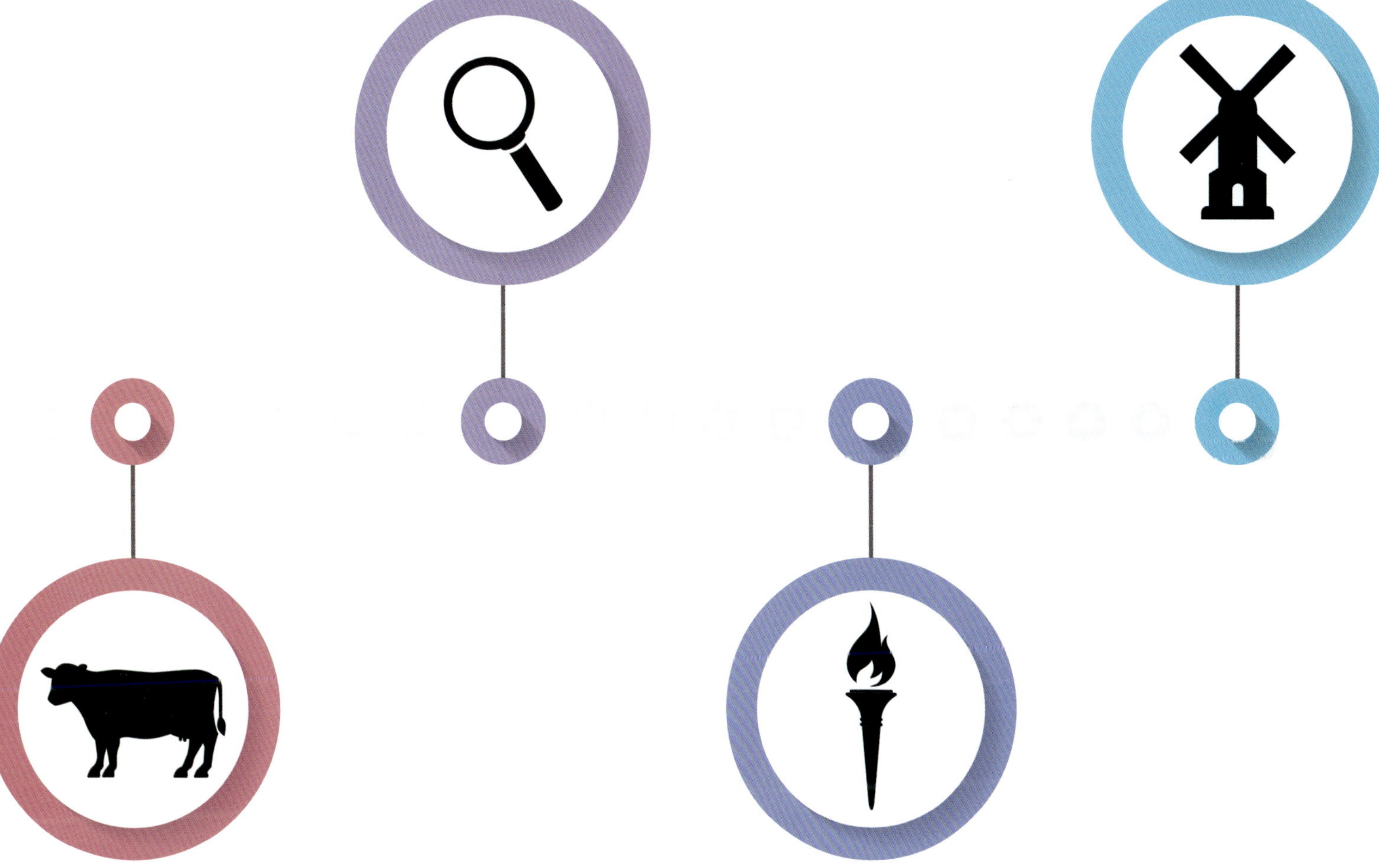

**3RD–1ST MILLENNIUMS BCE**

Working animals such as cattle, horses, donkeys and water buffaloes began to be used across the world.

**3RD CENTURY BCE**

Sunlight and mirrors used to light torches and, according to numerous ancient writers, Roman ships that were attacking the Hellenic city of Syracuse.

# THE INDUSTRIAL REVOLUTION

The Industrial Revolution changed everything. Before the Industrial Revolution, burning wood was the main source of energy generation. But wood supply could not keep up with demand. A more efficient and readily available energy source was needed. The answer was coal.

The heat from burning coal was used to make iron, which in turn was made into the machines that powered the factories – all of which were driving the speed and spread of the revolution. Coal was also used to power the steam engines in trains and steamships that carried coal and other products from Great Britain to the rest of the world.

*Steel manufacturing plant, circa 1918*

Large-scale coal mining spread from Great Britain to mainland Europe, North America and other parts of the world. By the early 20th century, coal was being mined on every continent except Antarctica. Coal mining during the Industrial Revolution was dangerous work that employed children, some younger than 10 years old.

The Industrial Revolution meant that more energy was required for manufacturing. This led to people investigating other sources of energy and how these sources could be used.

*A post-Industrial Revolution city showing pollution, circa 1926*

# WIND

*Renewable*

*Primary source of energy*

*First used by humans in the 4th millennium BCE*

***For:** less damaging to the environment than traditional energy sources such as fossil fuels; inexhaustible supply*

*Found everywhere*

*Forms instantaneously*

*Can be used in its natural state to make energy*

***Against:** wind supply can be unreliable*

Wind is air in motion. The energy from wind can be used to produce electricity by using turbines. As wind pushes on the turbine blades, the blades spin and turn a rotor, which is connected to a generator. This movement is then converted into electricity.

There are two main types of wind turbine: horizontal-axis (HAWT) and vertical-axis (VAWT). HAWT, such as those in the main picture below, are the most common and produce the majority of wind power around the world. Their blades must be pointed into the wind, they can be used on land or water, and they can be up to 260 metres tall.

In 2019, wind energy became the largest source of clean energy in Australia. It is renewable, its use creates zero toxic emissions or contaminates, and wind is available everywhere.

*Horizontal-axis wind turbines near Albany, Western Australia*

*Vertical-axis wind turbines*

# SOLAR

*Renewable*
*Primary source of energy*
*First used by humans in the 7th century BCE*
***For:** free; abundant; clean form of energy*

*Found everywhere*
*Forms instantaneously*
*Can be used in its natural state to make energy*
***Against:** supply of sunlight can be unreliable*

Solar energy is used to generate power by either thermal energy or photovoltaic energy. Thermal energy is made when sunlight heats up solar collectors. These devices contain air, water or other fluids. The materials they contain are heated and then used to warm buildings or for hot water systems, or to power steam turbines that make electricity.

Photovoltaic energy is made when sunlight reacts with photovoltaic cells, also known as solar panels. These devices convert sunlight into electricity by a process known as the photovoltaic effect. They can be used on homes or in large-scale power plants known as solar farms.

Australia has great potential for solar energy: sunlight. However, only a small amount of Australia's total energy consumption is made up of solar energy. Solar energy is naturally abundant and renewable, there are no greenhouse gas emissions and it can save money on energy bills.

*Solar energy farm near Townsville, Queensland*

# NUCLEAR

*Non-renewable*
*Primary source of energy*
*First used by humans in the 20th century*
***For:** reliable; affordable; abundant*

*Found in the Earth's crust, and in rocks and sediments*
*Present since Earth's formation*
*Can be used in its natural state to make energy*
***Against:** isolated cases of catastrophic failure that are harmful to humans and the environment*

Nuclear energy is found inside the nucleus of an atom. Changing the structure of an atom generates huge amounts of energy. This can be achieved in one of three ways. ***Nuclear fusion*** is when subatomic particles run into each other and form a bigger subatomic particle, releasing energy in the process. ***Nuclear fission*** is when the nucleus of an atom is split into two or more parts, releasing energy in the process. ***Radioactive decay*** is when the nucleus of an atom loses energy and turns into a different nucleus.

Nuclear fusion takes place within the Sun, with hydrogen atoms fusing to form helium. This type of reaction cannot be replicated on Earth. Nuclear fission, however, can be. The chemical element uranium is used as fuel and its atoms forced to split. Once they split, a chain reaction is started that makes heat, which is then used to make steam that powers turbines that make electricity.

Despite being one of the largest producers of uranium, Australia has never generated its own nuclear energy. This is partly due to its large reserves of fossil fuels and historical opposition to nuclear weapons. However, nuclear energy could be a potential answer to ensuring energy security and fighting climate change. Supporters believe nuclear energy is safe, reliable and affordable. Opponents are afraid of power plants failing and the resulting harm to nearby human populations and the environment.

*Inside a nuclear power plant cooling tower*

# FOSSIL FUELS

*Non-renewable*
*Primary source of energy*
*First used by humans in the 4th millennium BCE*
***For:** low cost; abundant; simple to convert into energy*

*Found in the ground; can be shallow or deep*
*Take millions of years to form*
*Can be used in their natural state to make energy*
***Against:** damaging to the environment; will run out*

Fossil fuels are the decomposing remains of plants and animals that lived long ago. Over millions of years these remains were covered in layers of soil and rock, compressing them and turning them into three different energy sources: oil, coal and natural gas.

Fossil fuels have been the most commonly used sources of energy since the Industrial Revolution. When oil, coal and natural gas are burned they release heat. This heat can be used to make steam, which then powers turbines that generate electricity. Fossil fuels can also be transformed into other energy products such as petrol, diesel and kerosene.

Crude oil is extracted by drilling deep into the ground. This can be done on land or at sea. The oil is then pumped to the surface or flushed to the surface with water. Coal can be mined at the surface or deep underground. Natural gas is most commonly extracted by drilling deep into the ground, and less commonly by fracking or acidising. ***Fracking*** is when high-pressure water, sand and chemicals are injected into rocks to break them apart. ***Acidising*** is when chemicals are used to dissolve rock and make the gas easier to reach.

Fossil fuels currently supply almost 80% of all energy needs worldwide. This is because they are low cost, easy to extract, and produce large amounts of energy. However, extracting and burning them is harmful to the environment.

*Pump jacks or "nodding donkeys" are used to lift oil up and out of the ground*

# FROM SOURCE TO YOU

Secondary sources of energy, such as electricity and petrol, go through many stages of production before they are ready for use.

Here is an example of how electricity can be made from primary sources of energy, such as fossil fuels.

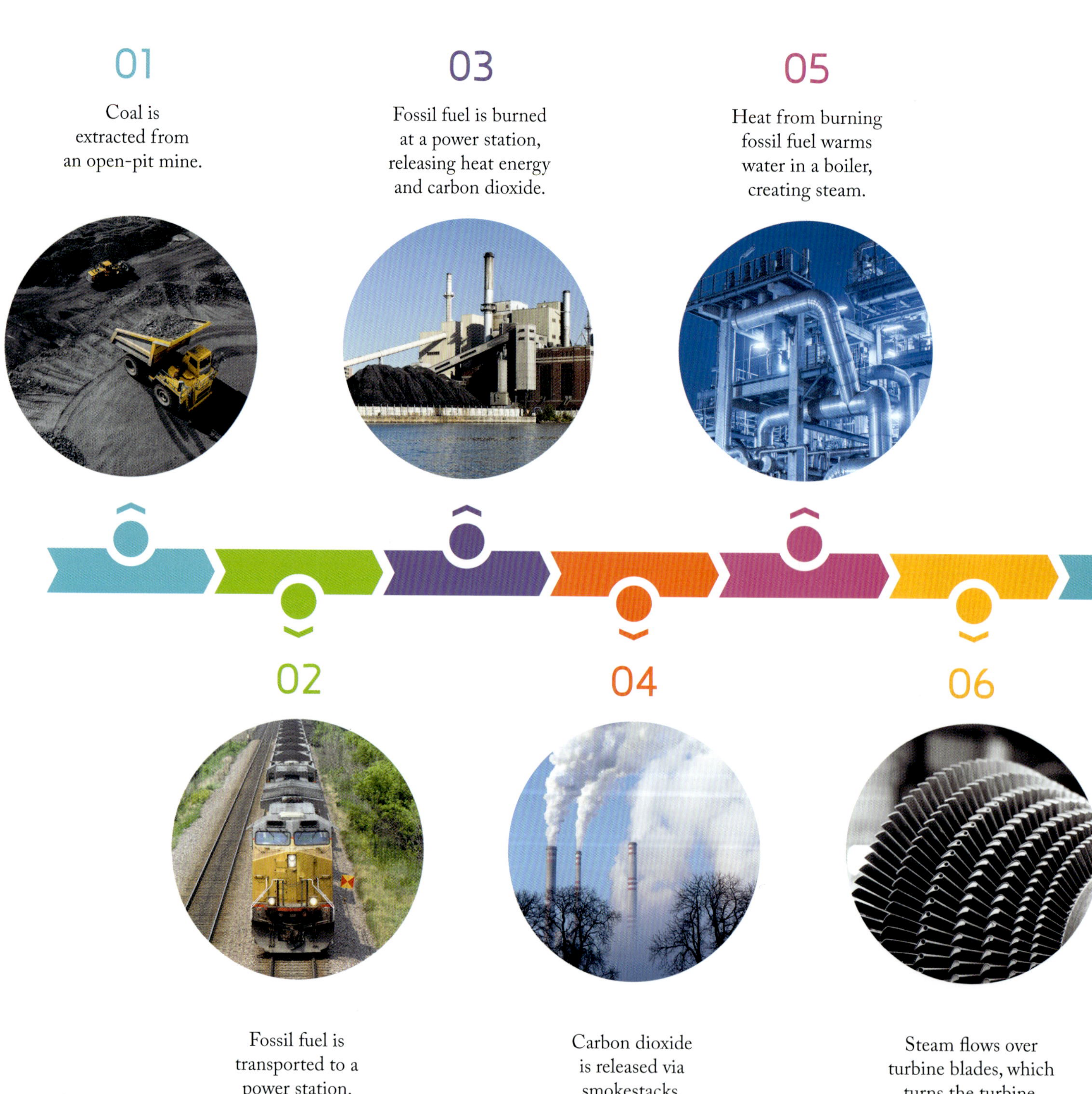

07

Motion of turbine spins a generator, which creates electricity.

08

Electricity is boosted to high-voltage via a step-up transformer at the power station.

09

High-voltage electricity travels to a substation via cables held up by large pylons.

10

At the substation, electricity becomes low-voltage via a step-down transformer.

11

Electricity is distributed from substation to homes by above-ground power lines or underground cables.

12

Electricity voltage is reduced via a step-down transformer.

13

Safe-to-use electricity is available in homes and is accessible from power outlets.

# $H_2$ HYDROGEN

*Renewable*
*Secondary source of energy*
*First used by humans in the 19th century*
**For:** *abundant; clean form of energy*

*Naturally present in water and hydrocarbons*
*Forms instantaneously*
*Pure hydrogen has to be separated from other compounds*
**Against:** *making pure hydrogen requires fossil fuels, which damages the environment*

Hydrogen is the simplest and the most abundant element in the Universe. It combines with oxygen to form water, and with carbon to form organic compounds known as hydrocarbons. These important compounds are used to make industrial products.

Hydrogen creates energy when it is burned in combustion engines. NASA has used hydrogen fuel to launch space shuttles into orbit since the 1970s. Hydrogen can also make electricity when it reacts with oxygen in a fuel cell. However, hydrogen does not occur naturally on Earth in large quantities and has to be made by separating it from other compounds. The two main ways of doing this are ***reforming***, which is when heat is applied to hydrocarbons; and ***electrolysis***, which is when an electrical current is passed through water.

Hydrogen energy produces no harmful emissions when consumed. But some of the processes used to make hydrogen rely on fossil fuels that release large amounts of carbon dioxide and carbon monoxide into the atmosphere. Hydrogen energy is also expensive and can be dangerous to use as a gas fuel because it is highly flammable.

*Launch of the space shuttle Discovery*

# HYDROELECTRICITY

*Renewable*
*Primary source of energy*
*First used by humans in the 4th to 2nd centuries BCE*
***For:** efficient; clean form of energy*

*Can be sourced in rivers and dams*
*Forms instantaneously, though dependent on rainfall*
*Can be used in its natural state to make energy*
***Against:** high cost; damaging to the environment; restricts the natural flow of waterways*

Hydroelectricity is generated by moving river water, typically by blocking the flow of rivers with large structures known as dams, which force water to collect into reservoirs. Controlled release of dam water can then be used to power turbines that make electricity.

Hydroelectricity can also be generated by water that has been pumped 'upstream' from a lower dam to a higher dam in a process known as pumped hydro energy storage (PHES). This method creates a water 'battery' and is done when there is excess energy available from other sources or when demand for energy is low and the energy is cheaper.

Hydroelectricity is used in 160 countries and provides about 16% of the world's electricity. In Australia it creates between 5% and 7% of all electricity supply and about 40% of all renewable energy.

Hydroelectric energy does not use fossil fuels and creates no harmful emissions. It is also more reliable and efficient when compared to solar, wind and coal. However, dams are expensive to build and they can be harmful to local plant, animal and human populations. They also rely on rainfall, and during droughts will produce less energy.

*Gordon Power Station in Tasmania*

# BIOMASS

*Renewable*
*Primary source of energy*
*First used by human ancestors in the Palaeolithic*
***For:** reliable; reduces waste*

*Can be sourced from trees, crops, garbage and landfill*
*Takes years to form, though regenerates in a person's lifetime*
*Can be used in its natural state to make energy*
***Against:** high cost to build; can be bad for the environment*

Biomass energy, like fossil fuels, is obtained by burning once-living plants and animals. But instead of taking millions of years to create, biomass can be grown and used to make energy within a person's lifetime. It has been used since prehistoric times, ever since people learned to use wood for fire.

Today, biomass can be used as a source of heat, such as wood in a fireplace. Biomass can also be burned in large power plants, with the resulting heat used to create steam, which then powers turbines that generate electricity. Biomass can also be converted into liquid and gas fuels.

Key types of biomass used in energy production include wood and agricultural products (crops, logs, woodchips, sawdust, crop waste and food processing waste); solid waste (garbage); landfill gas and biogas (methane from landfills and sewage plants); and alcohol fuels (ethanol and biodiesel). Biomass is currently responsible for about 1% of Australia's energy production.

*A biogas plant, which turns biomass into fuel*

# GEOTHERMAL

*Renewable*
*Primary source of energy*
*First used by human ancestors in the Palaeolithic*
**For:** *reliable; clean form of energy*

*Found deep in the Earth; at the Earth's surface*
*Forms instantaneously*
*Can be used in its natural state to make energy*
**Against:** *high cost to build; not available everywhere*

Geothermal energy comes from heat within the Earth. Humans bathed in geothermal hot springs as early as the Palaeolithic. It wasn't until the 20th century that geothermal energy was first used to generate electricity.

Geothermal power plants drill holes deep into the ground. Hot water is then pumped to the surface and converted into steam, which then drives turbines and generators that make electricity. After the steam cools and condenses into water, the water is pumped back into the ground. These power plants are usually in areas close to hot springs, geysers and volcanoes. In Australia, these areas are too far away from towns and cities where the power is needed, making building a power plant financially unviable.

*A geothermal power plant in Iceland*

# TIDAL

*Renewable*
*Primary source of energy*
*First used by humans in the 5th century CE*
**For:** *reliable; predictable; abundant*

*Sourced from ocean tides*
*Forms instantaneously*
*Can be used in its natural state to make energy*
**Against:** *expensive; may be harmful to the environment*

Tidal energy comes from the rise and fall of ocean tides, which are caused by the gravitational pull of the Sun and Moon. Tidal energy was first used to make large-scale electricity in the 20th century.

Tidal energy creates power in a way that is similar to wind turbines. Moving water flows over turbine blades connected to a rotor, causing the blades and rotor to spin. The rotor is connected to a generator, which converts the mechanical energy into electricity.

Unlike some other renewables, tidal energy is more predictable and reliable. Australia has no large-scale tidal energy production, though our large tides and extensive coastline suggests they could have great potential.

*A large tidal turbine ready for installation*

# WAVE

*Renewable*
*Primary source of energy*
*First used by humans in the 18th to 19th centuries CE*
***For:** reliable; abundant; clean form of energy*

*Sourced from ocean waves*
*Forms instantaneously when there is wind*
*Can be used in its natural state to make energy*
***Against:** high cost; materials prone to failure; may harm marine life*

Wave energy comes from the motion of ocean waves. Scientists have been researching wave energy technology for over 200 years, though it wasn't until the 21st century that commercial wave farms first appeared.

Ocean waves are most commonly made by wind. They can range in size from tiny ripples to tsunamis that are 30 metres tall. Wave energy is harnessed by floating devices known as wave energy collectors (WEC). These may be located close to shore or in deeper water where the waves are stronger. A generator converts the kinetic energy of waves into electricity, which is then transported to land by an undersea cable.

There are challenges to making wave energy. Less money has been spent on wave energy research compared to other renewable energy sources. Building devices for ocean use is expensive, and little is known about their impact on marine life. The effects of salt water and wave force means the devices wear out quickly and fail. However, wave energy has enormous potential. Oceans cover 70% of the Earth's surface. It is a powerful energy source that is clean, renewable and reliable.

*Ocean waves contain huge energy potential*

# CLIMATE CHANGE

Climate change is the change in weather conditions over a long period of time. This includes average temperatures, temperature extremes, rainfall, snow and sea ice levels, wind, and ocean activity. Climate change is also referred to as global warming.

Throughout Earth's history there have been periods where average temperatures rose and fell in a regular pattern over many thousands of years. This was usually because of small changes to Earth's orbit around the Sun. Since the Industrial Revolution, and since the middle of the 20th century, Earth's climate has been warming at an increasingly faster rate. This is mostly due to human activity and, in particular, extracting and burning fossil fuels.

When fossil fuels are used to create energy, a by-product is carbon dioxide. This gas, along with methane, nitrous oxide, ozone and water vapour, are collectively known as greenhouse gases. When these gases escape into Earth's atmosphere they act as a blanket, trapping radiant heat from the Earth that would otherwise escape into space. The increase of carbon dioxide and other greenhouse gases in the atmosphere has led to a rapid increase in average temperatures on Earth. Widespread logging and deforestation has made this problem worse, as forests and plants naturally absorb carbon dioxide through the process known as photosynthesis.

The effects of climate change are significant. Higher ocean temperatures mean more powerful cyclones. Longer periods of warmer weather cause polar ice sheets to melt faster and ocean levels to rise. Higher ocean levels cause coastal erosion. Bushfire seasons become longer and more extreme. Drought conditions worsen and impact food security. Rainfall and flooding increase. Animal habitats and breeding cycles are affected. Coral reefs become heat-stressed and die.

It is vital that we change our energy habits and rely less on fossil fuels and more on clean, renewable sources of energy.

EARTH'S ATMOSPHERE

GREENHOUSE GASES

Burning fossil fuels contributes to climate change, which will lead to increasingly severe hot and cold temperature extremes.

As Earth's average temperatures increase, more and more polar and sea ice will melt. This will lead to rising sea levels.

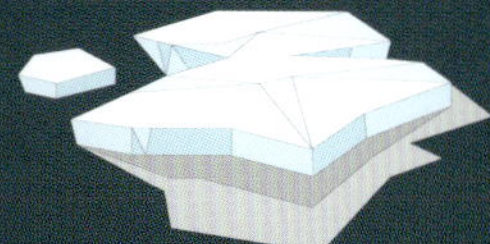

Rising sea levels will cause flooding and coastal erosion, while higher global temperatures will warm the oceans and cause more frequent and destructive cyclones.

As average temperatures on Earth increase, droughts will become longer and more extreme.

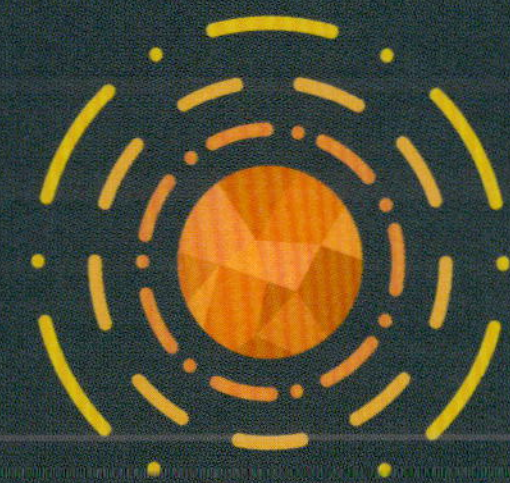

Extracting and burning fossil fuels is harmful to the environment and leads to more pollution in our atmosphere.

Climate change impacts animal habitats, while also affecting animal breeding cycles. This will ultimately lead to reduced animal populations.

# THE FUTURE OF POWER

Energy usage has increased enormously since the Industrial Revolution. Fossil fuels continue to provide the majority of this energy. Renewable energy sources such as wind, water and solar have become increasingly important, but they are not yet as reliable or on a scale that can fully replace fossil fuels. This means fossil fuels will still be used in the near future. But to address the problems of climate change, we must move quickly towards renewable energy.

The technology behind some renewable energy is becoming cheaper and more effective. Wind turbines are taller and their blades longer so they can catch more wind. They are also being designed to spin at lower wind speeds so they can generate power more consistently, and equipped with sensors that constantly react to wind information to improve their efficiency. Advances in solar energy include robots that change the position of solar panels to improve yield; building roads with materials that harvest solar energy; and the use of melted salt which allows some solar farms to make electricity day and night.

Energy sources being developed include:

- converting radio waves into energy
- using the chemical element thorium as a fuel in nuclear reactors, which produces less radioactive waste that is harmful to the environment
- space-based solar power farms within the next decade

Smaller scale sources of energy also being developed:

- turning human movement from playgrounds, nightclubs and gyms into electricity
- transforming onion juice into methane
- using body heat from train commuters to heat buildings
- converting livestock poo into electricity

Marine solar farms are being used, and research is being done to develop the potential of wave and tidal energy. Hydrogen energy could one day be produced on the same scale as oil and gas while also producing fewer emissions.

Nuclear energy, thought by many to be too dangerous to consider, may one day be the answer to solving our energy crisis.

A cleaner energy future means fewer greenhouse gases in our atmosphere. The rate of global warming will reduce and the effects of climate change will become less severe. Polar ice will have a chance to recover. Human, plant and animal health will improve, and there will be less hardship caused by extreme weather events. Earth will become a safer and happier place for everyone who calls it home.

# GLOSSARY

**absorb** to take in
**abundant** existing in large amounts
**ancestor** a relative from long ago
**appliance** a household device that runs on gas or electricity
**atmosphere** the whole mass of air that surrounds the Earth
**atom** the smallest particle of an element
**biomass** organic materials used as fuel
**combustion** the process of burning something
**commuter** a person who travels to and from work
**compound** a substance formed when the atoms of two or more elements join together
**consume** to use
**convert** to change into a different form
**crude oil** oil as it exists in the ground
**current** a flow of electricity
**decompose** to become rotten; decay
**deforestation** the action of clearing a large area of trees
**dissolve** when a solid mixes with a liquid and becomes part of that liquid
**efficient** achieving desired results with minimal waste
**element** a basic substance made up of atoms of only one kind, and which cannot be broken down into simpler substances
**emission** the production and discharge of something, such as gas or radiation
**erosion** the process of being worn away, such as by wind or water
**essential** extremely important
**exertion** physical effort
**extract** to remove something by force
**finite** limited in amount
**flammable** something that is easily set on fire
**force** the push or pull on an object
**fundamental** of central importance
**generate** to produce or create
**generator** a machine that produces electricity
**geothermal** heat produced inside the Earth
**geyser** a hot spring that shoots columns of water and steam into the air at irregular intervals
**habitat** the environment where an animal or plant naturally lives or grows
**harness** to control and make use of something for a particular purpose
**impurity** an unwanted substance found in something else
**inexhaustible** unable to be used up completely
**inexpensive** cheap
**infrastructure** the basic equipment and structures needed for something to properly function
**instantaneously** happening very quickly; at once
**kinetic** relating to the movement of physical objects
**logging** the business of cutting down trees for their wood
**motion** the action or process of moving
**nucleus** the central part of an atom
**photosynthesis** the process by which green plants and some other organisms use sunlight to turn water and carbon dioxide into food
**physics** the branch of science that deals with matter and energy
**plentiful** abundant
**potential** having the ability to develop into something more useful or successful in the future
**predictable** future events or behaviours that are able to be told in advance
**preserve** to prevent from decaying
**pylon** one of a series of tall, metal structures that supports long stretches of electrical wire
**radiant** transmitted by radiation, which is the emission of energy in electromagnetic waves
**revolution** a sudden and extreme change in the way people work and live
**rotor** a part of a machine that rotates around a central point
**sediment** material such as stones and sand that is carried by wind or water and deposited somewhere else
**subatomic** smaller than an atom
**thermal** relating to heat
**thorium** a chemical element with atomic number 90; a radioactive metal
**toxic** poisonous
**unviable** unable to be done successfully

# INDEX


Albany 16
Antarctica 15
Aristophanes 13
Athens 13
Australia 16, 17, 18, 23, 24, 25, 26
biogas 25
biomass 6, 7, 24
carbon 7, 22
carbon dioxide 7, 20, 22, 28
carbon monoxide 22
China 12, 13
climate change 5, 18, 28, 29, 30, 31
*Clouds, The* 13
coal 6, 7, 12, 14, 15, 19, 20, 23
crude oil 6, 19
*Discovery* (space shuttle) 22
Egypt 12, 13
electricity 6, 10, 16, 17, 18, 19, 20, 21, 22, 23, 24, 25, 26, 27, 30, 31
engine 6, 14, 22
Europe 15
fossil fuels 6, 7, 16, 18, 19, 20, 22, 23, 24, 28, 29, 30
generator 6, 16, 21, 25, 26, 27
geothermal 6, 7, 25
Gigawatt 11
global warming 28, 31
Gordon Power Station 23
Great Britain 14, 15
greenhouse gas 17, 28, 29, 31
helium 18
Hellenic Empire 13
horizontal-axis wind turbine (HAWT) 16
hydrocarbon 22
hydroelectricity 23
hydrogen 18, 22, 31
Iceland 25
Industrial Revolution 14, 15, 19, 28, 30
Iran 13
Iraq 13
Joule 10, 11
Kilowatt 10
Megajoule 10
Mesopotamia 12
natural gas 6, 7, 19
nodding donkeys 19
non-renewable 7, 18, 19
North America 15
nuclear 6, 7, 18, 30, 31
oil 6, 7, 12, 19, 31
oxygen 22
Palaeolithic 24, 25
pumped hydro energy storage (PHES) 23
primary source 6, 16, 17, 18, 19, 20, 23, 24, 25, 26
pump jacks 19
Queensland 17
renewable 7, 16, 17, 22, 23, 24, 25, 26, 27, 28, 30
Roman Empire 13
rotor 6, 16, 26
secondary source 6, 20, 22
solar 6, 7, 17, 23, 30, 31
Syracuse 13
Tasmania 23
thorium 30
tidal 26, 31
Townsville 17
turbine 6, 16, 17, 18, 19, 20, 21, 23, 24, 25, 26, 30
uranium 18
vertical-axis wind turbine (VAWT) 16
water 6, 7, 23, 26, 30
waterwheel 13
Watt 11
wave (radio) 30
wave (water) 7, 27, 31
wave energy collector (WEC) 27
Western Australia 16
wind 6, 7, 12, 16, 23, 26, 27, 28, 30
windmill 13